FROM SAIL TO STEAM

THE FINAL DEVELOPMENT AND PASSING
OF THE SAILING SHIP

BY

H. MOYSE-BARTLETT, M.B.E., M.A.

Non-members may obtain copies at 1s. 1d. each (post free), and members may obtain extra copies at 7d. each (post free) from the office of the Association, 21, Bedford Square, London, W.C.1

FROM SAIL TO STEAM

FROM the time when primitive man first went adrift on a bundle of reeds or learnt to balance himself on a floating log, to the days when his descendants, no more than a few generations ago, raced scrambling aloft to trim the towering sails of a full-rigged ship, the skill of the sailor remained the same : the application of the forces of nature in wind, tide, current and human muscles to the propulsion of his craft. Throughout this long period, although the principle involved remained unaltered, the ingenuity of man brought about a number of developments of even wider scope and more far-reaching importance than in the case of travel on land. Prior to the seventeenth century the record of such changes, especially as regards the ships of merchant traders, is imperfect and incomplete. The evidence available, however, is sufficient for a broad outline of the principal stages in the evolution of the sailing ship, an understanding of which is a necessary preliminary to any account of its last and most famous days.

Ancient Britain abounded in well-timbered river banks, so her earliest craft were dug-out canoes. By a crude process of pegging extra pieces of wood along their edges to secure greater freeboard, these evolved into plank-built boats, of which the original canoe became merely the heavy keel. Before the coming of the Romans the Britons probably used plank-built vessels similar to those of the Veneti, as described by Cæsar. Boats of skin stretched over wooden frameworks were also in use in southern England.

The early vessels of Northern Europe owed nothing to Mediterranean influence. Such evidence as we have shows that the ships of the Scandinavian seafarers differed in several important particulars from the contemporary Mediterranean galley. Bow and stern were similar in the Viking ships ; steering was effected by a single paddle on the starboard quarter instead of by double paddles ; clinker building, i.e. with overlapping planks, was the method of construction as opposed to the Mediterranean carvel building with flush planking. An interesting feature of the later type of Viking ship lies in the thorough understanding shown of underwater hull design to reduce resistance in the water. No such practice is apparent in the design of medieval sailing ships, and it was not until comparatively recent times that the principle was again scientifically applied in ship construction.

The earlier Norman ships appear to have differed little from the Scandinavian. The Bayeux Tapestry (c. 1120), however, affords evidence of a development which, though simple in itself, was of considerable significance. The Tapestry shows vessels of a clinker-built type, propelled by oars and by a square sail set on a single mast, and in a few instances what are apparently shrouds. These do not appear previously on any known representations of ships. So long as a vessel was expected only to run before the wind, shrouds would not be necessary, and their appearance, therefore, is indicative of a real advance in the practice of navigation, enabling advantage to be taken of a beam wind.

With greater dependence on wind and less upon oars, the fine lines of earlier craft disappeared, and for some three hundred years the average length of ships remained at about three times their beam. There was not as yet any difference between ships designed for war and those intended primarily for trade, though fighting-castles fore, aft, and on the mast, which eventually became permanent features of construction, were originally erections for the accommodation of soldiers. During the thirteenth century the bowsprit (the original purpose of which was to enable the bowline to be carried further forward) and the stern-rudder, made their appearance in Northern Europe. These two innovations carried the evolution of the sailing ship a stage further. As a result of the former, the windward leech of the sail was held taut so that the vessel could sail closer to the wind. The latter made the ship more easily controllable when sailing with a strong wind on the starboard quarter, which had hitherto been difficult or even impossible, as the heeling of the ship tended to lift the old starboard side-rudder right out of the water. With these improvements the vessels of Northern Europe can fairly be described as ships, for such craft required considerable skill in handling.

From the fifteenth century onward, progress in the art of ship construction was rapid. By far the most important development was the adoption of more than one mast. The two-master, essentially a Mediterranean type, never became popular in Northern Europe, perhaps because the balance of the ship was upset, as the mainmast was still stepped in the same central position as before. The earliest representation of a three-masted ship appears on a seal of Louis de Bourbon, dated 1466 ; the first three-masters cannot have appeared much earlier. They carried a large square sail on the mainmast, a small square sail on the foremast, and a " lateen," a triangular sail that had become very popular in the Mediterranean during the ninth century, on the mizzen. To this rig there was added later in the century a small spritsail, the function of which was to keep the ship's head off the wind. The three-masted ship, with its greater powers of manœuvre and its ability to sail with the wind on the beam as well as to take full advantage of a favourable breeze, thus became sufficiently handy to navigate all the waters of the globe. A variety of reasons contributed to bring about the great era of maritime exploration that began in the fifteenth century, but one of the main reasons why this development began when it did lay simply in the adoption of two extra masts in the medieval ship. Vessels of this type made possible the voyages of Vasco da Gama, Columbus and Magellan.

The maritime activity of the Tudor period resulted in a steady increase in the size of ships, and the adoption of a greater keel-length and finer lines. At this time the size of ships was calculated solely as a measurement of carrying capacity, either as " tons burden " (capacity when carrying wine in barrels) or as " tuns and tunnage " (capacity in bulk cargo, a somewhat higher figure). On this basis, the merchant ship of the period probably did not as a rule exceed 400 tons, though the royal ships were often considerably larger. The increase in the proportion of length to beam was seen in the " galleon," distinguished also by its projecting beakhead in place of the old, lofty forecastle. Under Henry VIII the warship became a separate type, owing to the king's insistence on the mounting of heavy guns capable of smashing the hull of an opponent, which led to the supersession of clinker by carvel building, and necessitated other modifications in design to ensure added strength. The heavy arming of merchant ships, making them sometimes practically indistinguishable from men-of-war, did not come until later, during the period when English merchants were engaging in unofficial wars in distant waters against their continental rivals. Meanwhile a more elaborate sail-plan was introduced including topsails and even topgallant-sails on the larger ships.

Tudor ships were usually decorated with painted designs on their upper works and with carved figureheads, but the era of elaborate decoration really began with the big three-deckers of the Stuarts, which were famous for their carved and gilded stern galleries. So lavish was the decoration of the *Sovereign of the Seas*, built out of the proceeds of ship-money in 1637, that it actually amounted to a fifth of the total value of the ship. An order of 1703 attempted to check such extravagance, at any rate so far as the royal ships were concerned, but the movement was a reflection of the nation's intense pride in its maritime strength.

Throughout the seventeenth century there was a steady movement towards finer lines, and a continuous elaboration of sail-plan and rig. Owing principally to the interest and industry of Samuel Pepys our knowledge of such developments is placed on a much sounder basis with respect to the post-Restoration period. But it must be remembered that the improvements thus recorded in the large warships of that time were only very slowly followed by the smaller merchant ships.

Early in the eighteenth century the steering-wheel replaced the whipstaff, or pivoted vertical lever that for nearly two hundred years had been used to move the tiller. During this century the dimensions of the different classes of men-of-war were standardised, and showed a steady increase in size. But the most important development was the great elaboration of the sail-plan. The forward part of the lateen yard and the lateen sail that projected beyond the mizzen were cut away, so that the yard became a gaff and the sail a " spanker," or " driver " ; jibs and staysails became common, and topgallantsails on all three masts. By the end of the century the full-rigged ship carried nearly forty sails. The larger merchant ships were by then very similar to men-of-war, though built on more generous line to secure greater cargo capacity and without the characteristic " tumble-home " that narrowed the top deck of the warship to preserve stability in view of its heavier armament.

The long series of naval wars that began in the middle of the eighteenth century and ended in 1815 was responsible for a notable advance in the speed, size, and manœuvrability of the sailing-ship. During the nineteenth century she was destined to come to her finest, fastest, and most beautiful form in the clipper. By that time, however, the new principle of mechanical propulsion was already well established. Throughout the nineteenth century there can be traced three parallel movements : the final, splendid evolution of the sailing ship, brought about by an unprecedented demand for fast passages that had its origin in the abolition of old trade monopolies and the growth of new colonies ; the replacement of wooden by metal hulls ; and the development of the steam engine, first as auxiliary, then as dominant partner, and finally as superseder of sail.

At the close of the Napoleonic War there were three main types of English merchant vessel. Those of the East India Company, which were generally built to a stereotyped naval pattern, though somewhat roomier and designed rather for comfort and for carrying capacity than for speed (a matter of secondary importance to a company in possession of exclusive trading rights), had then attained an average size exceeding 1,300 tons. At this time the company was running a fleet numbering more than a hundred vessels, chartered as a rule from private owners, who were often themselves members of the company. The West Indiamen, engaged principally in the important sugar trade with the West Indies, were much smaller, usually between 300 and 500 tons. The only other ships built in any numbers with a view to a particular class of trade were those engaged in the east coast coal traffic, which embraced also the major Baltic ports. These vessels were smaller still.

The loss of the East India Company's monopoly, which freed the trade with India in 1813 and with China in 1834, was followed by a period of intense commercial activity which in its turn brought about a major development in the construction of merchant ships. The new competition in eastern commodities led to a demand for fast passages ; speed suddenly became no less important than capacity. The best-known ships of the new type evolved to meet this demand were those constructed at the Blackwall shipbuilding yard, which had been in existence since the early years of the seventeenth century. Since the time when the first ships had been built there by Henry Johnson, a cousin of Sir Phineas Pett, this yard had been responsible for the construction of many famous East Indiamen, and now, with the growth of a demand for a faster type of ship, it began producing hulls of much finer lines than ever previously attempted in the construction of large merchant vessels. The " Blackwall Frigates," as they were usually called, attained a proportionate length of 4·7 in relation to beam, and as successors to the Old East Indiamen proper, continued to hold the regular passenger and cargo trade with eastern waters until the century was well advanced. They retained their characteristic stern windows and quarter galleries long after these features had disappeared from other types.

In the early years of the century the eastern trade was of far greater importance than that of the Western Ocean, which had not yet recovered from the effects of the American War of Independence. When it did revive, it remained for some time almost entirely in the hands of American sailing companies. The Black Ball Line began the first regular service between New York and Liverpool in 1816. The Red Star, Swallow Tail, and Dramatic Lines on the same route, and the Black Cross Line on the route between New York and London, followed soon after. The keen element of competition introduced by the operation of so many rival companies was enhanced by the desire to secure the mail contracts. It was the captain, and not the company, who profited by the allowance of twopence (or two cents) a letter ; and it was the captain, rather than the ship, who was selected by the intending emigrant, anxious, since he had to provide his own food, to cross the Atlantic in the shortest possible time. So hard were these ships driven that only the most seasoned of Liverpool " packet rats " would willingly stand up to such conditions. The eastbound passage, usually accomplished in about half the time necessary for the westbound, was reduced in a very short time from an average of three weeks to less than a fortnight. Thus on the western as well as the eastern runs the early years of the century witnessed the rise of a competitive demand for fast passages on a scale previously unknown in the history of sail. At the height of the emigration boom following the middle of the century a passage to America could be bought for as little as three pounds ten shillings.

The result was the production for the first time of a class of merchant vessel designed primarily for speed. The Americans led the way with the *Ann McKim*, built at Baltimore in 1832. This ship was copied and improved upon until by the eighteen forties the real clipper (of which the first is usually held to be the *Rainbow*, built at New York in 1845), with her distinctive bow, modified stern (which slipped through the dead water instead of holding it), high proportion of length to beam—rising eventually to as high a figure as 6·7—and her imposing array of between thirty and forty sails, including such extra devices as skysails and studdingsails, brought the full-rigged ship to the peak of perfection. After the repeal of the Navigation Laws such vessels began to appear in English waters in increasing numbers in search of trade.

The cession of Hong Kong as a free port after the Anglo-Chinese War of 1839–42 and the opening of Shanghai to foreign trade in 1843 encouraged still further the growth of the eastern trade. The quality of tea was considered to deteriorate while in the hold of a ship, and amid the growing demand for still faster passages the American clippers found their opportunity. The first to break into this trade was the *Oriental*, launched in 1849 at New York, a clipper that set up a record on its first voyage from the Far East by acomplishing the passage to London from Hong Kong in ninety-seven days. The Blackwall Frigates stood no chance against such opposition, and British shipowners began ordering clippers from American yards. But the British yards were not slow in producing clippers of their own. In 1850 Green of Blackwall built the *Challenger* and Hall of Aberdeen the *Stornoway*, which in the following year made two fast passages, of 102 and 103 days, to Hong Kong. Similar ships followed, still faster and finer in their lines. During the next twenty years many records were made and broken in the famous tea-race from China. Comparisons of alleged records must always be examined with care, and the resulting conclusions sometimes accepted with reservations, for at this period there were no " recognised courses " such as that now admitted for the Atlantic Blue Riband. The many claims put forward by owners on behalf of their ships are not always the best means of assessing their qualities under sail. But the spectacular tea-race gave rise to a good deal of interest. One of the most exciting of these races took place in 1866 between the *Ariel*, *Taeping* and *Serica*, all built by Steele of Greenock. They left Foo-chow-foo together, and docked in London on the same tide ninety-nine days after. Still faster passages were recorded before the opening of the Suez Canal finally drove the clippers from the China trade altogether.

The Australian gold rush of 1851 offered another opportunity of which the American clippers attempted to take advantage. Within sixty years of the discovery of gold, nearly a quarter of a million people emigrated to Australia, creating a demand for shipping that could only be met by resort to extraordinary measures. Tonnage was diverted from the eastern trade, bought on the American market, and ordered urgently both from American and British yards. A problem no less serious was the provision of crews, who developed a tendency towards wholesale desertion in Australian ports. Special precautions were necessary to keep them aboard, particularly at Melbourne, and it was not unknown for ships to make the homeward passage with crews brought up to strength with convicts drafted from Australian prisons.

Much of this emigrant trade lay in the hands of the Liverpool shipowners, among whom James Baines, owner of the Black Ball Line, was particularly active. Before the rush the passage to Australia had usually taken about four months, but with three American-built ships, the *Marco Polo, Lightning* and *James Baines,* he successively lowered the record to sixty-three days. The last-named ship is reputed on one occasion actually to have exceeded for a short while a speed of twenty knots.

As the gold rush died down the importance of the Australian trade was maintained by the development of exports of timber, gum, hides, tallow and, above all, wool. Here also there was a particular motive in desiring fast passages, for wool sales were held in England on fixed dates, and the wool clippers often left Australia with the express intention of catching them. As the tea trade passed into the hands of the new steamship companies, many of the China clippers were diverted to the Australian run. Famous passages were made by the *Thermopylæ, Sir Lancelot,* and *Cutty Sark,* the last-named averaging over eight knots on her best voyage, for the tea clippers were as a class generally faster than the wool clippers, though their smaller capacity was a drawback in handling so bulky a cargo.

The introduction of metal hulls was a factor of considerable importance in enabling Britain to maintain her maritime position in the face of serious challenge from abroad. From the days of the earliest sea-going craft of the Egyptians, with their hogging-truss of twisted rope passing under bow and stern and over Y-shaped posts on the centre line, the provision of latitudinal strength had constituted one of the main problems in the construction of wooden ships of any size. If a certain length were exceeded, the vessel was very liable to break her back, especially in rough weather or on going aground. Sir Robert Seppings made an effort to solve this problem by introducing a system of diagonal framing into the construction of wooden warships. But added strength was only gained by this method at the cost of a certain clumsiness that materially reduced sailing speed, and it was evident that the solution to the problem, and with it the possibility of a substantial increase in the size of ships, must lie elsewhere.

Although it was early recognised that an iron pot would float just as easily as one made of wood, it was for long contended that an iron ship could not prove satisfactory on the grounds that it would be far too heavy and cumbersome for easy handling. Actually, iron construction resulted in a saving of more than a third in weight, while enabling more sail to be carried in a head sea without fear of straining the ship. Iron was tried for shipbuilding soon after the Napoleonic War. In 1829 the famous shipbuilder John Laird of Birkenhead launched his first iron ship, and during the next decade his lead was followed in other yards, for any development conducive to hard driving was sure of serious trial. These were sailing ships; it was not until 1837 that the first iron sea-going steamer appeared, the *Rainbow*, of 600 tons. It soon became apparent that a stranded vessel could be refloated without serious damage in circumstances that would have resulted in the total loss of a vessel made of wood. One of the principal advantages enjoyed by American yards in their keen competition with British shipbuilders during the middle of the century was a handy supply of plentiful timber. It was in an endeavour to counteract this advantage that many of the new British clippers, laid down especially to compete with their American rivals, were constructed of iron. These clippers owed their speed not only to their longer lines, which exceeded those of the American softwood ships, but also to their proved ability to stand the strain of hard driving in heavy seas.

The introduction of iron hulls was a movement affecting the development of sailing ships and steamers alike. On certain routes in tropical waters, however, there was an intermediate stage before iron vessels generally replaced those of wood. One of the earliest problems confronting traders to countries such as China and Australia was the fouling of the hull. The only effective (though very expensive) remedy lay in sheathing the vessel below the water-line with copper or yellow metal. The use of iron nails to secure the copper had been found impracticable on account of the corrosion caused by electrolytic action between the two metals when immersed in salt water. In consequence it was at first held that iron vessels would be useless in the China trade, since their hulls could not be sheathed. To overcome this disadvantage a type of building known as "composite" was evolved, the iron framing of the ship being covered with planks, and these again with a copper sheath secured by copper nails. Eventually the introduction of anti-fouling preparations made such devices unnecessary; copper sheathing fell into disuse, and composite building went with it.

The success of iron hulls was productive of advantages to British shipping more far-reaching than mere technical improvements in design and speed. In the middle of the century, just

9

at the time when British shipowners were feeling the increasing effects of American competition, the Irish famine brought about the repeal of the Corn Laws, and also the suspension of the Navigation Laws in order to accelerate the rapid importation of grain. In February, 1847, a committee was appointed to examine the system. There followed an immediate outcry from shipowners all over England, led by the Shipowners' Society of London. It was argued that British shipping owed its success mainly to the operation of these laws ; that the bulk of the British carrying trade would inevitably fall into foreign hands ; that a decrease in shipping would undermine our naval supremacy by weakening trained reserves. In spite of these arguments, the bill passed its readings in the Commons, though with a dwindling majority, and the Navigation Laws were repealed in June, 1849. The immediate result was undoubtedly a setback to British shipping, which suffered a temporary decline. The situation was restored, however, by the unusual demand for shipping created by the Australian gold rush and the Crimean War, followed later by the withdrawal of American competition as a result of the Civil War. But recovery was also assisted by another factor, the influence of which has not been so generally recognised : the replacement of wooden by iron ships in a country which, although poor in timber, possessed what was at that time the most highly-developed iron and steel industry in the world. Thus the lean years were tided over. The general adoption of iron hulls was followed by the introduction of iron masts and spars, and, of still greater importance, steel rigging. During the eighties steel hulls also came into general use, lighter by some fifteen per cent. than those made of iron. Owing to the early development of steel processing in Britain, this still further increased the advantage enjoyed by British shipyards. The first ocean-going vessel built of steel was the *Rotomahana*, launched in 1879.

The demand for fast sea passages created by the rapid expansion of trade and emigration in the nineteenth century was at first met chiefly by developments in the design of sailing ships. It was many years before the marine steam-engine offered a serious challenge to the clipper, and it is a source of some gratification to ship-lovers that the full-rigged ship was able to reach such heights of beauty and speed before being driven from the seas by the rise of mechanical power. At first regarded as of no more value than to propel a tug, the steam-engine gradually won recognition as a convenient asset for manœuvring in narrow waters. Then came a stage when sail was auxiliary to steam as a useful means of saving coal when winds were particularly favourable. By the end of the century the steamship had triumphed by practically ousting the full-rigged sailing ship from every important trade route on the seas.

The first British steamer went noisily afloat in 1788, when William Symington fitted a two-cylinder engine to a twenty-five-foot boat and attained a speed of five knots on a Scottish loch. In 1802 he produced his second effort, the *Charlotte Dundas*, which was driven by a large paddle-wheel aft and met with some success towing boats on the Forth and Clyde Canal. Similar experiments were in progress in America at about the same time. The first steamboat to carry passengers in this country was the *Comet*, of twenty-four tons, which appeared in 1812. She was described in her owner's advertisement as "a handsome vessel to ply upon the River Clyde from Glasgow, to sail by the power of air, wind and steam," a feat accomplished by the use of a three horse-power one-cylinder engine and of a large square sail, set on the funnel. Her career ended eight years later, when she went ashore at Craignish Point. In 1815 the *Marjory*, a paddle-steamer of seventy tons, began a similar service between London and Gravesend, to be quickly followed by several others. So far the new invention had been confined to inland waters, as the uncertain machinery and flimsy paddle-wheels were not considered capable of withstanding the rough usage of the open sea.

But the experiment was soon made, and made successfully. In 1816 the first sea-going steamboat, the lugger-rigged *Hibernia*, began a service between Holyhead and Ireland. Within the next five years there was a rapid increase in steam tonnage. Properly speaking, however, these early cross-Channel boats were not steamers at all, as they were built on the same lines as sailing ships, and, of course, carried one or more sails, either on masts or on the funnel. The real distinction began when David Napier, after a series of experiments with models, introduced the wedge-shaped bow. The effectiveness of steamers having been proved on short voyages in home waters, it was not long before some of the more enterprising shipowners began experimenting with steam on the Atlantic passage. It is hardly possible to give an exact date for the first crossing of the Atlantic under steam, but auxiliary engines were used as early as 1819, when the *Savannah* made a passage from New York to Liverpool. Most of the voyage was made under sail, but her engines were in use until the fuel ran out, as testified by her captain's entry in the log of "no cole to git up steam" as the vessel approached the British Isles. During the course of the next twenty years many similar passages were made by other sailing ships fitted with auxiliary engines, which were used for varying periods in accordance with the type of weather encountered. The most popular sail-plan for these early steamers was the barque rig. Their engines were of the beam type, with low-pressure boilers ; paddle-wheels were in any case unsuited to the application of high pressures. For many years the difficulty of stowing an adequate supply of coal strictly limited the use of engines.

It was obvious that much work must be done on the development of the marine engine before steamers could hope to break the monopoly of the fast sailing packets operating along the Atlantic routes. But the crossing is, after all, comparatively short. Sailing ships, however hard driven, could only advertise their date of departure ; the date of arrival could never be forecast with any certainty. So far as passenger traffic was concerned, reliability, if it could be ensured, might prove an even greater attraction than speed.

The first serious attempt to attain this object on any scale did not come until 1838, when the *Great Western* of 1,320 tons made her maiden voyage. She was constructed especially for the North Atlantic passenger service, and fitted out on a lavish scale. There were actually bells in the staterooms to summon the stewards. Such efforts to improve conditions of travel were long overdue, though some time was still to elapse before the matter was brought under proper control. Passengers were still too often regarded as necessary evils rather than the basis of the owner's profits. Those wealthy enough to pay for staterooms were sometimes forced to provide bedding and even furniture. Steerage passengers were usually supplied only with water and fuel, and received no other service whatever. During the great emigration rush of the fifties, which brought into the passenger trade many ships totally unsuited for the purpose, serious overcrowding aggravated these evil conditions until it was not unknown for steerage passengers to die of hunger, when a particularly bad passage made them too ill to cook or swallow their dwindling supplies of food. Improvement began in earnest with a series of laws to regulate the emigrant trade, one of the most important of which was the Passenger Act of 1855, which gave wide powers to emigration officers to check overcrowding and secure arrangements for proper feeding. The enforcement of these regulations afterwards became the duty of the Board of Trade.

Perhaps the chief impetus towards the early establishment of regular steamer routes lay in the competition to secure the mail contracts, on account both of the financial rewards and the constant effort and efficiency needed to ensure fulfilment of the contract terms. The success of the *Great Western* and of two similar ships, the *British Queen* and *President*, in making more regular passages than the sailing-packets led the British Government to issue an invitation for tenders. The contract went to a new undertaking, specially formed to secure it by Samuel Cunard of Halifax, Nova Scotia. The original fleet of what came eventually to be known as the Cunard Line numbered four wooden steamers of over 1,000 tons, the *Britannia, Acadia, Caledonia* and *Columbia*. Within eleven years nine more ships, successively larger and more powerful, were added to the fleet, and provided a service of weekly sailings. This service was not established without provoking strenuous competition from America. The subsidised American Collins Line, which came into existence in 1850, began running an excellent fleet of five steamers. But two of these were lost at sea, and with the withdrawal of the subsidy in 1858 the Collins Line ceased operations.

Early competition with sailing ships on the longer eastern routes offered a more difficult problem. On the Cape route the cost of providing coal at intermediate stations was at first prohibitive ; even on the shorter Mediterranean route, which was broken by portage across the Suez Isthmus, it was an expensive undertaking. None the less, the East India Company very soon showed its interest in the new development, for the matter was under consideration as early as 1822. Here again mail contracts played an important part, and led to the offer of a grant by the company for the establishment of a steamer service by either route, held to be successfully accomplished after two round voyages, with a maximum of seventy days allowed for the passage.

In 1825 two vessels, the *Enterprise* and the *Falcon*, both fitted with engines, left for Calcutta. The latter used her engines so little that her passage could hardly be considered a genuine attempt. The former, a paddle-steamer of 479 tons register, spent 103 days at sea. She was purchased by the company and employed with success on the Calcutta-Rangoon service. This experiment was followed by the use of river steamers on the Hughli and Irrawaddy, and further trials with steam on the run between India and China. Some of the later Blackwall Frigates, such as the *Vernon* and *Earl of Hardwicke*, were equipped with engines and paddle-wheels, but they depended chiefly on the fact that they were full-rigged ships, and generally used their engines for brief periods only.

In spite of early disappointments, the East India Company continued to persevere. During the thirties a steamer service was started between Bombay and Suez. It was expensive and irregular, though less affected by the monsoon than the former service run by sailing ships, and provided timing of arrivals and departures was reasonably accurate, made the Mediterranean-Red Sea route unquestionably the quickest way to India. In 1837 a mail contract was secured by the Peninsular Steam Navigation Company, which for three years had been operating between London, Spain and Portugal. In 1840 the company added two new steamers to its fleet, changed its name to Peninsular and Oriental Steam Navigation Company, and extended its service to Malta and Alexandria. In 1842, in spite of opposition from the East India Company, which maintained its Suez-Bombay service until 1854, the P. and O. inaugurated a new service between Suez, Madras and Calcutta with a large new paddle-steamer, the *Hindostan*. The result was a considerable improvement in the passage between this country and India, and an increase in the number of passengers electing to travel by the Mediterranean route. This was reflected in the added provision made for their comfort on the overland portion of the journey, for which they had originally been required to make their own arrangements. Anything up to 3,000 camels might still be needed for transporting the cargo of a single vessel, but for passengers camels and donkeys were replaced by horses and two-wheeled carriages ; river transport was arranged where practicable ; and after 1843 a chain of hotels and rest-houses was organised at staging posts. Similar improvements continued up to the time when it became evident that the long-discussed canal was about to become a fact. But there were always some passengers who preferred the more leisurely journey round the Cape.

Within a few years further mail contracts had enabled the P. and O. to extend its services to the Far East, running at first to Penang, Singapore and Hong Kong, and later to Shanghai, Swatow and Amoy. Other steamer lines followed, such as the Calcutta and Burma Steam Navigation Company, which began carrying mails for the East India Company in 1857, and later, under its present name of British India Steam Navigation Company, absorbed most of the coastal trade of India, the Persian Gulf and the east coast of Africa. Meanwhile an attempt by the P. and O. to establish a service with Australia was temporarily suspended owing to the Crimean War, but was resumed later in competition with the Royal Mail Steam Packet Company, both concerns running services that eventually included Sydney, King George's Sound and Melbourne. Several attempts were also made during the early fifties to run steamers to Australia via the Cape, but it was as yet too early for the steamer to challenge successfully this final stronghold of the clipper. Difficulties enough were still experienced over coal supplies on the other route, where the P. and O. employed over two hundred sailing colliers annually to supply its needs. It was not until the opening of the Suez Canal on 17 November, 1869, that the success of the steamer on the Far Eastern and Antipodean runs was fully assured, at the expense of the regular lines of sailing ships to China and Australia. Fewer than five hundred ships passed through the Canal during the year following its completion, but this number was nearly trebled in the next five years, and went on increasing steadily as steam tonnage multiplied. One by one the sailing-ship companies running to Australia and New Zealand turned over to steam, or retired from the contest. The Orient Line became the Orient Steam Navigation Company in 1878, and began a fortnightly service to Australia in conjunction with the Pacific Steam Navigation Company. The latter was succeeded for a time in the service by the Royal Mail, until the Orient Line bought out other interests and assumed responsibility for the Australian mails on its own. The Aberdeen Line began replacing its clippers with steamers in 1881. A similar policy was followed a few years later by a new company formed from the amalgamation of the old Shaw, Savill and Albion Lines.

In a region so vast and remote from organised fuel supplies and repair workshops as the Pacific, it might be expected that the sailing ship would have remained unchallenged by steam until the century was well advanced. In 1840, however, owing to the efforts of an American named William Wheelwright, who had failed to obtain the necessary support for the project in his own country, a royal charter was granted to the Pacific Steam Navigation Company for the operation of a service " along the shores of North and South America in the Pacific Ocean." The Company started with two small paddle-steamers of about 700 tons, the *Chili* and *Peru*. Here again mail contracts helped the Company through its early struggles. For a time the service was confined to the Pacific coast. In 1865 it was extended to the River Plate, via the Falkland Islands, and three years later a direct service, that before long consisted in regular fortnightly sailings, was inaugurated between the Pacific coasts and England.

But it was the Western Ocean runs that were responsible for the real development of the steamer. A year or so after the foundation of the Cunard Line, the Royal Mail Steam Packet Company, which had come into existence in 1839, obtained a contract for carrying mails to the West Indies, Mexico and the former Spanish Main. Fourteen steamers were soon in use on this service, which was of so onerous a nature that the company was for many years in financial difficulties. However, the contract was renewed in 1850, and the company extended its service to Rio and the River Plate. During the next twenty years many more steamship lines appeared on the Atlantic routes : the Inman Line to the United States, which was soon engaged in a healthy rivalry with the Cunard Company ; the Allan Line to Canada ; Alfred Holt to the Caribbean ; the African Steamship Company to the West African coast ; and the Union Line, which secured the Cape mail contract in 1857, four years after its foundation.

During the latter half of the century competition between steamship companies, especially on the Atlantic routes, grew very keen. In 1867 a new White Star Line succeeded to the house-flag of a line of sailing ships that had borne the same name. This company entered the Liverpool-New York service in 1871 with a new steamer, the *Oceanic* of 3,707 tons. Within five years four more ships, the *Adriatic, Celtic, Britannic* and *Germanic* had been added to the fleet, and a new service was being developed in the North Pacific between San Francisco, Japan and China. By concentrating on the provision of better accommodation, especially for steerage passengers, the company soon became well established, and was the first to instal gas-plants for lighting, though the experiment did not prove a success.

The rapid multiplication of new steamship lines during the two decades that followed the middle of the century was the outcome of a great stride in marine engineering. The advantages of the streamlined hull were not confined to clippers, and in steamship design followed the introduction of the wedge-shaped bow. Constant improvements in the manufacture of iron and steel made possible the construction of tubular boilers, capable of withstanding high pressures, and the development of the expansion engine, in which steam was expanded successfully in more than one cylinder. The use of this type of engine, which was tried out as early as 1854 in the steamer *Brandon*, resulted in greater economy in fuel, reduced the stress on bearings, and gave greater regularity to the turning movement. Experiments were somewhat protracted, but triple-expansion engines came rapidly into use after 1880.

The most important improvement, however, was the invention of the screw propellor. The advantages of a screw over the more vulnerable and clumsy paddle-wheels had long been realised, but there were certain practical difficulties to be overcome in the design of stern and rudder to permit of proper steering without undue interference from the screw, and in the casting of bearings sufficiently hard to withstand the constant wear of the shaft. In 1837 experiments by Francis Smith with a thirty-foot boat on the Paddington Canal gave promise of commercial success, and two years later the first screw-propelled sea-going ship, the *Archimedes*, of 232 tons, was launched by a syndicate formed for the purpose. As a result of her success the Great Western Steamship Company in 1843 fitted their new steamer, the *Great Britain*, of 3,500 tons, with a screw instead of paddle-wheels. On her maiden voyage across the Atlantic she averaged nine and a half knots.

At this time steamers on the Western Ocean routes did not exceed four thousand tons, and were usually smaller. In 1858 an experiment was made that gave rise to such interest that its importance has since been greatly exaggerated. This was an attempt, with the launching of the *Great Eastern*, of 18,914 tons, to discover whether a vessel so very much larger than anything previously built would prove more economical than several smaller ones. She was built on the longitudinal system, with transverse bulkheads separating her into compartments each sixty feet in length. In addition to carrying sails she was propelled both by screw and paddles, under the power of which she could steam at fifteen knots. Valuable lessons in marine engineering were learnt during her construction, but commercially she was a failure. As her name indicates, she was originally intended for the eastern trade, but it was difficult to find a service on which she could profitably engage. After several transatlantic voyages she was employed in cable-laying in the Atlantic and Indian Oceans, and ended her career as a show ship before being broken up in 1890.

The screw propellor was the decisive factor in converting the Navy from sail to steam. At an early stage in the history of steam the Admiralty had acquired a number of small steam vessels for general purposes, but owing to the vulnerability of paddles, reliance continued to be placed on the old wooden sailing ship as a fighting unit. In 1843 the sloop *Rattler* was launched, a screw steamer of 1,078 tons. A tug-of-war was arranged between her and the *Alecto*, a paddle-steamer of approximately the same tonnage and power, in which the *Rattler* towed her opponent backwards at over two knots. The first warship designed as a steamer was the *Agamemnon*, launched in 1852. The Crimean War proved beyond doubt the obsolescence of the old line-of-battle ship. Wooden hulls gave place to iron at about the same time ; the last wooden warship, the *Victoria*, an auxiliary steamer of 121 guns, was launched in 1859. During the succeeding decade the first iron-clads, large vessels carrying no sails at all, made their appearance, though many years were still to elapse before cruising under sail disappeared from the Navy altogether.

The nineteenth century witnessed the rise and growth of a code of marine legislation that materially improved the conditions of merchant seamen. The disappearance of the East India Company's Maritime Service had struck a blow to the prestige of the mercantile marine. The tradition of this great seafaring service, with well over three hundred years' experience to its credit, was scattered after 1834, and only gradually rebuilt. " No respectable people send their children to sea now," remarked an old shipowner during the discussions preceding reform of the Navigation Laws, recalling sadly the days when the Maritime Service had been considered a fit occupation for the best families in the land. There was no lack of individual commanders who insisted on some measure of smartness and efficiency, but the realisation that apprentices could be used as a means of securing cheap labour contributed to a general lowering of the status of officers, and in most ships it was customary for the second mate to take his turn with the men in all but the most menial tasks. In the early years of the century the conditions under which the crews lived were often as bad as, or even worse than, in the days of Elizabeth.

In 1850 the first major act was passed for improving conditions and maintaining a proper discipline among merchant seamen.

Nine superficial feet of space was to be allotted to the accommodation of each member of the crew; a supply of medicine was to be provided; an examination was made compulsory for the masters and mates of all foreign-going ships; proper articles of engagement were to be drawn up, and regulations enforced to ensure a regular method of engagement and discharge. Another act passed four years later gave the Board of Trade chief control over maritime affairs with power to hold courts of inquiry into the circumstances of wrecks and vessels lost, and laid down a number of provisions dealing with the safety of life at sea. In 1870 Samuel Plimsoll, Liberal M.P. for Derby, took up the cause of merchant seamen in the House of Commons. The violence of his views undoubtedly led to a certain disregard for fact in his book, *Our Seamen*, published in 1873. But this did little to diminish its widespread influence, and Plimsoll secured a strong backing in the country, resulting in the incorporation of provisions for a compulsory loadline in the Merchant Shipping Act of 1876. After 1890 the position in which this " Plimsoll mark " was painted was no longer left to the owner's discretion. It must be remembered, however, that long before this time the Board of Trade had been empowered to prevent a ship from sailing if it was considered unfit to proceed to sea.

On the long ocean routes to Australia, New Zealand and the Pacific, for which the early paddle-steamers were unsuited and where coaling was expensive, the sailing ship continued in some measure to hold her own until the last decade of the century. For such trades the clippers had usually been built on somewhat roomier lines, and often exceeded 3,000 tons. By the late eighties they could no longer compete with steamships as a means of fast transport, and as they went out of commission were not replaced. For a time, however, the building of sailing ships continued for the Chile guano trade and for general cargo, and even experienced a revival in the four-masted barque, square-rigged on the fore, main and mizzen, and fore-and-aft rigged on the jigger. Speed being no longer the first consideration, all such extra aids towards the spread of canvas as skysails, studdingsails, and jib-booms disappeared. With them went the finer clipper lines, and the roomy barques of this period sometimes attained a size of well over 5,000 tons. Much romantic interest has centred on such of these ships as were still in commission during the present century, but to the sailor who remembered the heyday of the clipper they were no more than clumsy steel boxes. The last of these deep-sea sailing ships to fly the British flag was the *Garthpool*, launched as the *Juteopolis* in 1891. She remained in commission till 1929, when she was lost on the Ponta Reef, off the Cape Verde Islands.

A comparison of tonnage may serve as a broad illustration of the rate at which the supersession of sail by steam was accomplished. In 1829 nearly three hundred ships, totalling some 30,000 tons register, had been fitted with steam-engines. At mid-century, sailing ships totalled about $3\frac{1}{4}$ million tons, and steamers about 165,000. During the next twenty-five years sailing tonnage increased to well over 4 million. Steam tonnage was then less than half that figure, and did not equal sailing tonnage until about 1880. Sailing tonnage was by then declining at an ever-increasing rate until by the end of the century it accounted for no more than a quarter of the total British tonnage.

There is one aspect of the maritime progress of the nineteenth century that should not be overlooked. Owing to the rapid expansion of overseas trade and of colonisation, British oceanic policy became worldwide in intention and in fact. Our shipping was enabled to fulfil the requirements that this entailed by successive improvements in design, by a technical skill that developed the new inventions in propulsion, by an enterprising spirit that accepted financial risks and successfully overcame initial difficulties, and by the advantage enjoyed by Britain as a producer of coal, iron and steel. A further factor was the preoccupation of her only serious rival with domestic issues during the critical mid-century years. But behind all this lay a deeper, more far-reaching significance. From the time when its authority ceased any longer to meet with serious challenge during the Napoleonic War, British naval power assumed a position in world affairs far transcending the mere implications of what is known as "foreign policy." In the suppression of slavery, the policing of the seas to stamp out piracy, and the surveying and charting of distant waters, the Navy assumed an international rôle that came to be accepted by Englishmen as a part of its natural function. This could not have been accomplished had Britain failed to meet the growing demands made on her mercantile shipping after 1815. For naval power cannot be created by the mere voting of taxes ; nor can it flourish except on the basis of a sound seafaring tradition. This the Merchant Navy provided during the nineteenth century on an expanding scale commensurate with the needs of a growing Empire. Historians have stressed at length the exploits of Tudor and Stuart seamen in the history of British expansion, but similar influence on the growth of the Empire in more recent times is often too little regarded. To suppose that the maritime growth of the nineteenth century was no more than the necessary fulfilment of the law of supply and demand is not in accordance with the lessons of history : we need only to study the fate of Spain as a world power for ample proof that the needs of empire will not of themselves create that maritime strength on which the cohesion of the whole so largely depends.

Lightning Source UK Ltd.
Milton Keynes UK
UKHW040959131021
392137UK00001B/3

9 781447 411949